Table of Contents

I0004537

Preface

Talking to other people one-to-one makes up a significant proportion of the total amount of communication that you are involved in each day. Active listening will reduce the chance of misunderstandings, help to solve problems, and allow you to take advantage of opportunities you may have previously missed. This eBook describes what active listening is and how it can make you a more effective manager.

You will learn:

- Why it is so important to actively listen

- The six aspects of listener orientation you should adopt

- How to use reflection and clarification in the context of active listening

- How to overcome the internal barriers to effective active listening

- How to integrate different types of questioning into active listening

Introduction

The simplest example of interpersonal communication in the workplace is a conversation between two people. This activity makes up a significant proportion of the total amount of communication that you are involved in each day, and doing it well has a big influence on your effectiveness as a manager.

A deceptively simple concept called active listening can really help you to improve your communication skills. It was originally developed in the context of therapeutic interviews, but its principles can be applied to workplace communications.

Listening is the most fundamental component of interpersonal communication skills and is an active process in which a conscious decision is made to listen to and understand the messages of the speaker. As a listener, you should remain neutral and non-judgmental; this means trying not to take sides or form opinions, especially early in the conversation.

Active listening is concerned with improving your ability to understand exactly what the other party means when speaking to you. This is not as straightforward as it sounds because active listening involves listening for meaning (specifically, the meaning perceived by the other party), not just listening to the words they use and accepting them at face value.

Active listening requires patience because people need time to explore their own thoughts and feelings before putting them into words. This means that short periods of silence should be accepted and you need to resist the temptation to jump in with questions or comments every time the speaker pauses.

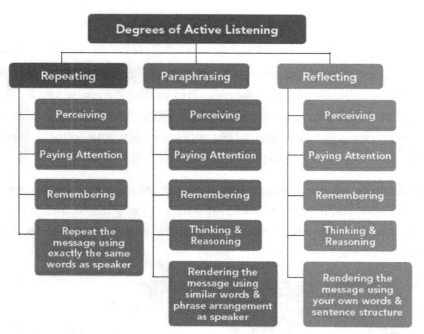

A listener can use several degrees of active listening, each resulting in a different quality of communication. The active listening chart above shows the three main degrees of listening:

- Repeating

- Paraphrasing

- Reflecting.

There is no universally accepted definition of active listening because its main elements were already in widespread use before clinical psychologist Carl Rogers popularized the term in 1957. Rogers described active listening from a therapeutic standpoint and his original definitions are not all that helpful in everyday workplace communications.

However, from a practical perspective, the essence of this skill is to put your own concerns, attitudes, and ideas to one side while you listen. Without these distractions you are able to observe all the conscious and unconscious signs displayed, enabling you to discern the true meaning behind spoken words.

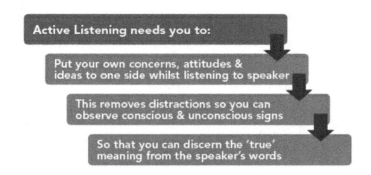

This technique leaves the speaker in no doubt that you are giving them your full attention and when it is used skillfully, active listening can:

- Demonstrate your undivided attention

- Encourage the other party to continue speaking

- Restart a completely stalled narrative

- Reassure the other party regarding self-disclosure

- Confirm, improve, or correct your understanding

- Fill any gaps in the content of the narrative

- Improve the other party's insight into the issues

- Build rapport between you and the other party

KEY POINTS

✔ Active listening is a straightforward technique that you can use to improve your communication skills.

✔ Active listening involves listening for meaning, not just listening to the words that are spoken.

✔ An active listener is neutral, non-judgmental, and fully engaged throughout the conversation.

✔ Active listening demonstrates your undivided attention, encourages the other party to continue speaking, and can build rapport and understanding between you and the speaker.

Characteristics of Active Listening

Any manager who can master the techniques of active listening will be able to have a more productive and motivated team. This is because your team members will feel that they are listened to and understood. The atmosphere active listening engenders within your team means that they will be happy to contribute their views and ideas, creating a strong connection between members.

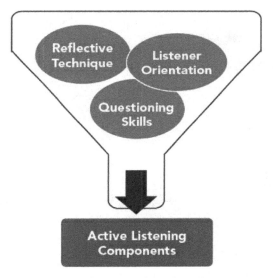

There are three components of active listening that you need to understand in order to master this essential communication skill. They are:

- Listener Orientation

- The Reflective Technique

- Questioning Skills

Listener Orientation

Successful active listening begins with you making a conscious effort to approach the conversation with a positive attitude to the other person and to the encounter itself. This means that the central question for you is not 'What can I do for this person?' or even 'How do I see this person?' but rather 'How does this person see themselves and their situation?'

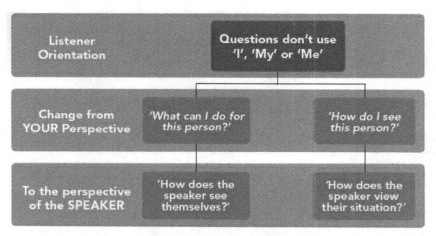

In his original paper on active listening, the clinical psychologist Carl Rogers felt that, for best results, the listener orientation should be characterized by undivided attention, empathy, respect, acceptance, congruence, and concreteness.

Undivided Attention

This should be self-explanatory: 100 percent of your attention is on the speaker. You need to make sure that any important communication takes place in an environment that is free of distractions and where you won't be disturbed. You should also switch your cell phone to silent and avoid looking at it, or at your computer screen, or anything other than the person you are listening to.

Empathy

Empathy begins with awareness of another person's feelings and develops naturally out of active listening. Obviously, it would be easier to empathize if the other party simply told you how they felt. However, unless you are dealing with someone who is unusually candid you will need to interpret nonverbal cues. You also need to pay attention to the precise language that they are using.

You can show empathy by acknowledging their emotions, whether these are positive or negative. For example:

'I can understand why you feel that way.'

The ability to empathize is critical, as it helps you to 'tune in' to the things that are important to the speaker. Empathy is surprisingly difficult to achieve because we all have a strong tendency to advise, tell, agree, or disagree from our own point of view.

Respect

This means thinking well of every person, rather than judging them according to a preconceived standard of personal worth. It does not necessarily mean agreeing with them, but it does mean that you should be respectful on a personal level, rather than dismissive or condescending.

Acceptance

Acceptance, in this context, is very close to the concept of respect, and again requires a non-judgmental approach. It means that you should avoid expressing agreement or disagreement with what the other person says. It is simply accepted as the current state of play and this will serve as a starting point for later discussion. This attitude encourages the speaker to be less defensive and to say things that they might otherwise keep hidden.

Congruence

This refers to openness, frankness, and genuineness on your part as the listener. This can be a problem if you have strong negative feelings about what you are hearing. For example:

> *If you are annoyed with someone it can be very difficult to show empathy, respect or acceptance.*

In this case your choice would be either to admit to feeling annoyed or to postpone the conversation until you have calmed down.

The first course of action may be the better one because honesty on your part will usually lead to the speaker opening up as well, rather than both of you communicating from behind a mask of false affability.

The principle of congruence is an important one because people are very good at reading each other's body language and para-verbal signals. This means that if what you say is at odds with what you feel then the other party will notice this and believe either that you are lying or confused. Generally speaking, these conflicting meanings leave the recipient suspicious or hostile, without quite knowing why.

Concreteness

This refers to focusing on specifics rather than vague generalities. For example, consider the statements:

> *'Supplier X is always late delivering.'*
> *OR*
> *'Supplier X has been more than one day late on three out of the last five de-liveries.'*

The first of these is a vague statement whilst the second is concrete. Often, a person who has a problem will avoid painful feelings by being abstract or impersonal, and will say things like:

'IT support seem to be a bit overworked.'
'The management need to get a grip on tasking.'

When what they really mean is:

'John Smith from IT support is not returning my phone calls.'
'I've got too much work and Jane is sitting around doing nothing.'

They may also depersonalize things by saying something like, 'I think most people want...' rather than 'I want.' You can encourage concreteness by asking them exactly who or what specific incident they are referring to.

KEY POINTS

- ✓ Listener orientation means making a conscious effort to approach the conversation with a positive attitude to the other person and to the encounter itself.

- ✓ It is characterized by undivided attention, empathy, respect, acceptance, congruence, and concreteness.

Reflective Technique

The second component of active listening is the reflective technique, which involves reflecting back to the speaker what it is you believe they mean. However, it also has a second major element, which is the clarification of the meaning of what has been heard. In practice, reflection and clarification are intertwined, in that reflection often leads to some degree of clarification, and attempts at clarification often require some degree of reflection.

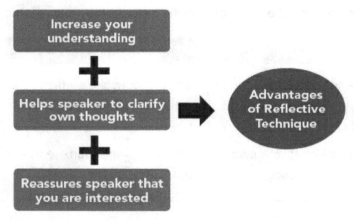

The advantages of this technique are threefold:

- It increases your own understanding

- It helps the speaker to clarify his or her own thoughts

- It can reassure them that you are interested in their point of view.

Reflection

The term 'restatement' is often applied to this part of the technique because it involves paraphrasing the speaker's words back to them as a question. For example:

> *Speaker: 'I don't think that's possible.'*
>
> *Listener: 'Are you saying that it's not possible to fulfill the order by Friday with the staff we have available?'*

The most important part of this approach is that it must take account of the speaker's nonverbal signs as well as the actual words they use.

When employing verbal reflection, shorter interjections have the advantage that they interrupt the low of the narrative less. Keeping your questions brief also forces you to stick to the main points, but it is not always possible because you do need to be specific rather than general.

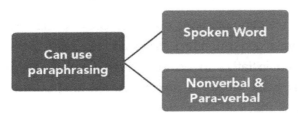

By using reflection, the speaker can see that you are paying attention to them and making a conscious effort to understand what they mean. If you want to do this verbally you can use phrases or supportive sounds such as 'Yes,' 'Go on,' 'Ah ha,' 'OK,' or 'Mm.' Altering your posture slightly (for example, moving forward) or nodding your head shows you are taking on board what they are saying. You can also use the appropriate facial expression or make eye contact to signal to the speaker you are listening to them.

This tends to encourage people to open up and make their case in an honest and heartfelt way. If you feel there is more to explore you can use paraphrasing of the last few words spoken or an open question to keep the conversation alive. In some instances you may just want to remain quiet in order to give the speaker time to gather their thoughts again. These simple techniques can help bring to light issues that you were previously unaware of.

Clarification

A mixture of reflection and direct questioning can get to the bottom of what people mean. These approaches enable you to correct misunderstandings and ill gaps in the narrative, thus gaining a better understanding of the overall situation.

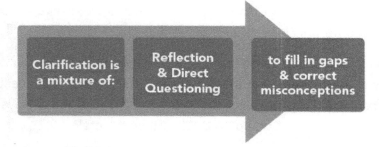

The process of reflection provides an opportunity for the speaker to point out inaccuracies in your understanding. However, you need to be aware that they may not take the initiative to do so. Consequently, you should pay close attention to their body language and be on the look out for nonverbal signs that might indicate that you have misinterpreted their meaning.

Another thing to be aware of is that you can only clarify information that the speaker has articulated. If you suspect that significant information is being withheld, you cannot reflect it in the usual way, because you don't know what it is. Instead, you have to somehow reflect its absence by asking questions that lead the speaker to bring it into the open.

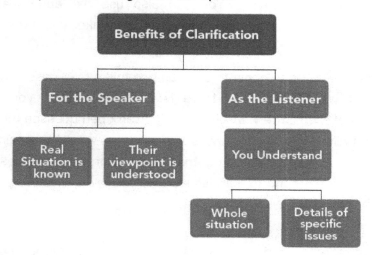

From your perspective, the end result of clarification is a fuller and more accurate understanding of the overall situation and a detailed understanding of specific issues. From the speaker's perspective, the end result should be a feeling that their circumstances and point of view have been understood.

Central to this process is the fact that you need to overcome any natural tendency that you may have to rush in with suggestions or solutions. If you do not, you will be unable to avoid acknowledging your own emotions during the communication. You need to allow the speaker to present the whole picture so that they expose the level of their knowledge and the extent of their ideas on how to address the issue in hand.

Some simple techniques you can use to ensure that you ask for clarification rather than offer your own opinion are as follows:

- State what you think the speaker has said, as you understand it

- Check whether this is what they really meant

- Use open, non-directive questions—if appropriate

- Ask if you have got it right and be prepared to be corrected

- Admit if you are unsure about what the speaker means

- Ask for specific examples where necessary or if helpful for understanding.

By allowing several seconds of silence before you ask a question or give feedback you will ensure that the speaker has said all they want to. You can also indicate your attentiveness by accurately paraphrasing the speaker's words into a statement that communicates your impartiality and comprehension. It also allows you to clarify that you have understood their explanation of the issue.

When using clarification, a significant part of the technique is your ability to summarize the whole communication exchange, thereby illustrating your understanding of what has been said. In your summary be concise, objective, and non-judgmental, using the speaker's frame of reference to describe the essential elements of your conversation.

Where this conversation is part of several discussions you will often use your previous summary at the beginning of your next conversation to refresh and restate your current understanding.

Principles of Clarification

Listen more than you talk

Respond to what is personal to the speaker

Reiterate only what speaker has said

Appreciate the sentiment of the speaker, not just facts

Respond with acceptance & empathy

KEY POINTS

- ✔ Reflection involves reflecting back to the speaker what it is you believe they mean.

- ✔ This technique increases your own understanding, helps the speaker to clarify his or her own thoughts, and can reassure them that you are interested in their point of view.

- ✔ A mixture of reflection and direct questioning can get to the bottom of what people mean.

- ✔ The principles of clarification are:

    - ✔ More listening than talking

    - ✔ Responding to what is personal rather than to what is impersonal, distant, or abstract

    - ✔ Restating and clarifying what the other has said, not asking questions or telling what the listener feels, believes, or wants

    - ✔ Trying to understand the feelings contained in what the other person is saying, not just the facts or ideas

    - ✔ Responding with acceptance and empathy, not with indifference, cold objectivity, or fake concern.

Questioning Skills

The third component of active listening is the art of questioning.

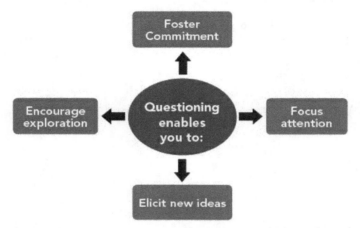

Developing your ability to ask questions that draw out the information needed to aid your understanding of the speaker's situation and help them find a resolution is crucial to your success. Your questions help you to:

- Focus attention

- Elicit new ideas

- Encourage exploration

- Foster commitment

There are seven different types of questions you can ask, and you should make sure that you have a clear idea of why you are asking a question in a particular way and at a particular time.

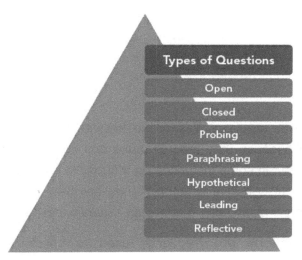

Open questions are commonly used to encourage the other party to open up, so that you can gather the necessary information. They often start with why, what, where, which, and how. You will find that they work best when the conversation is already lowing freely. For example:

> *'How was that strategy useful?'*
> *'What did you do to keep your team on track?'*
> *'How would you respond to this customer's concerns?'*

Probing questions can be used to clarify something that has already been said or to find out more detail about it. Many of them are helpful in creating rapport, but you must take care not over-use them as this can make people feel as if they are being interrogated or even attacked.

Make sure your verbal and nonverbal signs are neutral or supportive when asking such questions. This type of question is useful in uncovering details that may have initially been overlooked or thought irrelevant. For example:

> *'Why do you think this is the case?'*
> *'What does that mean?'*
> *'What are your options for solving the problem?'*
> *'Could you be more specific?'*
> *'Who is involved? Who are the key stakeholders?'*
> *'What needs addressing?*

'Is there an option that you have not yet considered?'
'How have you managed to put up with the situation to date?'
'How would an objective observer describe this situation?'
'What do you care most about in this situation?'
'What are your concerns?'

Closed questions require a *'yes'* or 'no' answer. Such questions should be used sparingly because they tend to make any conversation feel awkward and one-sided, but in some instances an affirmative or negative answer is all that is needed. In sensitive situations, they are best avoided as they can harm the rapport and empathy that are an essential part of active listening.

Reflective questions are frequently used to check and clarify your understanding. This style of question reflects back to the speaker what they have just said and allows them to fully explore their knowledge of a situation.

These questions also provide an opportunity for the other person to give voice to the emotions they felt at that particular time without you having to interpret why this happened in your question. Use of reflective questions dispenses with you having to express an interpretation or judge why the other person felt this way.

For example:

Speaker-'I feel frustrated with myself.'
Listener-'And what is this "frustrated with myself" experience like?'
Speaker-'Those people in dispatch are always messing me about'
Listener-'What does that "messing you about" behavior involve?'

Leading questions need to be used with care because they imply that there is a right answer to the question, which contradicts the ethos of active listening. They are useful in situations where you require a desired answer or need to influence people's thinking. For example:

'So wouldn't it have been better to...?'
'Don't you think we should have...?'

Hypothetical questions allow you to gauge how someone might act or what they think about a possible situation. They are effective in getting the person to think up and discuss new ideas or approaches to a problem. For example:

'What would you do if…?' '
What would happen if…?'

Paraphrasing questions are one of the best ways you can check your own understanding of what the speaker has said. For example:

Speaker-'I can't deliver on that unless accounts get the information to me the same day.'
Listener-'I'm hearing you say that you could deliver if the accounts department were able to get the information to you on the same day you requested it. Am I understanding this correctly?'

Whenever you ask a question think about how and where you are trying to 'take' the speaker. If the question you ask does not result in a positive step forward then you must ask yourself three simple questions: 'Did I ask it in the wrong way?', 'Could the words I used be misinterpreted?' and 'Was the type of question appropriate?' The answers you get by asking yourself these things will enable you to develop your questioning competency and alter your behavior in the future.

KEY POINTS

- ✓ Questions can help you to focus attention, elicit new ideas, encourage exploration, and foster commitment.

- ✓ There are seven different types of question you can use: open, probing, closed, reflective, leading, hypothetical, and paraphrasing.

Barriers to Active Listening

To use the active listening techniques effectively, you need to put your personal feelings aside during the conversation, ask questions, and paraphrase the answers back to the speaker. Some of the barriers that can prevent a proper understanding of the issues involved include physical and cultural factors such as a noisy environment, a strong regional accent, or a difference in terms of reference.

In addition to these external factors, which are usually fairly easy to overcome, there are some less obvious barriers that you should be aware of.

Inappropriate nonverbal cues

These include things like facing or leaning away from the other party, not maintaining eye contact, looking tense, or presenting a 'closed' posture by crossing your arms, etc. If what you say is being continually contradicted by your body language then there is no possibility of the other party opening up.

Your posture and gestures must always reflect that you are paying complete attention to the person speaking to you. Distractions force you to send inappropriate nonverbal signals to the speaker, and it only takes one such signal to destroy the benefits you can gain from active listening.

Taking the Spotlight

This refers to the tendency most people have to share equally in the conversation. It involves shifting from a passive role into an active one and effectively taking the focus of the encounter away from the other party and onto yourself. It can be difficult to avoid doing this once you feel as though you understand the issues involved.

Before you are tempted to take the spotlight remember that as soon as you begin giving advice or instructions you are no longer listening to the other party.

Stereotyped Reactions

When you are seeking clarification by using reflective questioning it is very easy to get into the habit of beginning your questions with phrases like:

> *'Are you saying that…?'*
> *'Do you mean that…?'*

If you are not careful with this type of questioning it can alienate the other party because it can sound patronizing. You should only use this type of reflective questioning when the meaning of something they have said actually *needs* clarifying.

Inappropriate Responses

If you are asked a direct question then the most appropriate response is usually to answer it rather than look for any deeper meaning. If the other party says

> *'When are we likely to get some extra resources?'*

The best answer is usually a direct one. For example:

> *'We're getting two extra people next week.'*
> *'I should know on Thursday.'*

You can then proceed to ask more questions if you genuinely need clarification of something, but you should try to avoid answering direct questions with a question of your own, because it can make you appear vague or evasive.

Pretending Understanding

If you really don't understand what the other party is trying to say then you should always seek clarification in a direct way—for example, by saying something like

'Sorry, I didn't get that. What are you saying?'

Hoping that their meaning will eventually become clear is unnecessary and undermines the whole process. If you're confused by something that has been said, then say so and ask for an explanation.

Overreaching and Under-reaching

Overreaching involves ascribing meanings that go far beyond what the other party has expressed, by stating interpretations that are conjecture on your part. Under-reaching involves missing the meaning of what has been said because it does not agree with your own view of how things are.

It can be tempting to seek confirmation of your own views and you may need to make a conscious effort to avoid doing so.

Long-windedness

Giving very long or complex responses breaks the low of the conversation and makes it less likely that you will gain an understanding of the other party's position. Short, simple responses are more effective.

KEY POINTS

- ✔ There are many barriers to active listening, including physical and cultural factors such as a noisy environment, a strong regional accent, or a difference in terms of reference.

- ✔ There are also barriers that you can create yourself if you are not careful. These include: inappropriate nonverbal cues, taking the spotlight, stereotyped reactions, inappropriate responses, pretending understanding, overreaching and under-reaching, and long-windedness.

Advantages for Managers

Active listening is a skill that can be acquired and developed with practice. However, active listening can be difficult to master and will, therefore, take time and patience. Used appropriately, active listening may provide three very positive results:

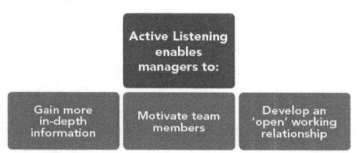

Firstly, the listener gains information because active listening encourages the speaker to talk about more things in greater depth than he or she would be likely to do in simply responding to directive questions or suggestions. Such depth of discussion often exposes underlying problems, including ones the speaker had not recognized previously.

Secondly, the elements of listening orientation (empathy, acceptance, congruence, and concreteness) are likely to increase as the reflective listening process continues. These are the ingredients you need for an open, trusting relationship with your team members.

Finally, active listening stimulates and channels motivational energy. As the listener, you accept and encourage the speaker, but you leave the initiative in their hands. Consequently, your team member will recognize new avenues for action and will begin making plans to pursue them, making themselves more effective and productive.

KEY POINTS

- ✓ Active listening enables managers to: gain more in-depth information, motivate team members, and develop an 'open' working relationship.

Summary

Active listening enhances your ability to absorb and pass on the data and information given during the exchange. By developing your skills and techniques to actively listen your communications will offer your listeners greater clarity and empathy.

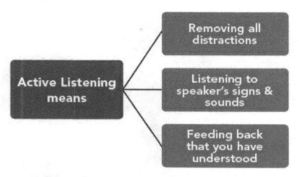

An essential aspect of active listening is your ability to block out any distractions that may be present where you are communicating. By giving 100 percent to your conversation you will hear and comprehend the true content of the message as well as being able to pick up all the unconscious signs displayed.

If your natural tendency is to rush into a response, practice taking a breath before you talk so that the other person has the opportunity to finish what they are saying. If don't do this and you cut off the person's response before they have explained their whole viewpoint you will not have a complete picture. Beware of this and the many other barriers you must avoid to gain the benefits of active listening.

Without the whole picture of the discussion you are more likely to misinterpret the exchange. To keep your focus on what is being said to you give the speaker signs that they have your full attention by slightly moving your head or eyes. You may also need to ask others in the situation to be quiet so the speaker can express themselves.

By behaving in this way you will be able to put together more persuasive replies and achieve your communication objective. It also illustrates your understanding of the speaker's viewpoint and how this relates to your own beliefs.

By paying attention to the other person's responses you will be able to accurately judge their topic knowledge and adjust your communication style appropriately. You also have the opportunity to feed back to the individual that you have comprehended what they are saying to you.

This makes them feel valued and willing to contribute further, and ensures the exchange is a two-way process. This can be achieved by simply following your summation of what they have said with such phrases as:

Does that make sense to you?
What do you think?
Would you agree?
What's your view on this?

In addition, you can encourage another person to make a contribution to your exchange by using a pause or remaining silent. This offers you two advantages. First, it gives you as the listener time to pull your thoughts together, and secondly, people have an innate desire to ill a void, so they begin to speak.

The two-way communication active listening encourages also provides you with the opportunities to give reasoned and valid feedback, as well as allowing you to gain clarification of what you believe has been said to you.

This is one of the techniques that enable you to minimize the distractions that can occur during an exchange or dialogue. Being able to retain the focus of the communication on your objective is essential for success. An important side effect of such behavior is that others will follow your lead when conducting their own communications.

By developing your abilities to use all three components of active listening—listening orientation, reflective technique, and questioning skills—you will be able to maximize the effectiveness and productivity of the individuals in your team.

www.ingramcontent.com/pod-product-compliance
Lightning Source LLC
Chambersburg PA
CBHW070929050326
40689CB00015B/3671